Classic Cocktails

TOP THAT!

Copyright © 2004 Top That! Publishing Inc,
25031 W. Avenue Stanford, Suite #60,
Valencia, CA 91355
www.topthatpublishing.com

Introduction

The history of the cocktail is somewhat blurred. All that can be said for certain is that mixed drinks, both alcoholic and non-alcoholic have been drunk throughout the world for hundreds of years

Predictably, claims for the origin of the word "cocktail" are accompanied by colorful and outlandish anecdotes. A popular story is that of Betsy Flanagan, an innkeeper during the War of Independence. She is said to have served American and French officers a meal of roast chicken, stolen from a nearby English farmer. The officers washed down their meal with drinks decorated with the bird's tail feathers, mocking their enemy with toasts of "vive le cocktail!"

Another story tells of a bar, where a large ceramic container in the shape of a cockerel was used to store the leftovers of drinks. The potent, if sometimes unpalatable mixture, was served from a

tap at the "tail" of the bird, hence the term "cocktail." Other theories are based upon anything from drunken fighting cocks to docked horse's tails — every cocktail aficionado will have their favorite story.

The Martini is generally agreed to be the first modern cocktail. The classic mix of gin and vermouth, garnished with a cherry or olive was popular across the USA by 1900. However mixed drinks really took off during prohibition. The illegal hooch produced by the bootleggers generally tasted awful, so recipes were concocted to make it more palatable. Cocktail favorites such as the Harvey Wallbanger and the Manhattan all date from this time.

The classic cocktail conjures up images of style, sophistication, and cool glamor. Exotic-tasting mixes remind us of holidays, frivolity, and fun. So try out these recipes and realize your own cocktail fantasy!

 page three

Equipment

**Making quality cocktails requires a
range of special bar equipment.
The cocktail shaker is essential.
Your need for the other items will
depend on the type of drinks you
make the most and whether or not
you are a stickler for detail**

Bar spoon

Long-handled spoons used mainly for
mixing drinks directly in the glass.
Also used for "muddling"—crushing
sugar, herbs or other ingredients

Blender

Used for blending frothy cocktails or
mixing in crushed ice. The tall, goblet
style blenders are best for cocktails

Cocktail shaker

The three-piece shaker has a base to hold
ice and a built-in strainer. The larger
Boston shaker can mix drinks more quickly,
but you will need a separate strainer

Corkscrew/bottle opener
No bar would be complete without this

Fruit squeezer
Freshly-squeezed fruit juices are
essential for certain cocktails

Measures
These are essential for measuring
amounts of alcohol

Mixing glass
A large glass beaker used to stir cocktails

Nutmeg grater
Does exactly what it says. Grates nutmeg
very finely to top off Eggnogs and
other frothy drinks

Strainer
Used with a Boston shaker to
separate the pips and fruit pulp
from the drink

Ice crusher
Used for crushing ice. Specialist
mechanical and electric ice crushers
are also available

Glasses

Good presentation is very much a part of enjoying cocktails. For some, only the correct glass will do, but you should use whatever you think looks good

(1) Champagne glass
The old-fashioned bowl is a very elegant and stylish way to serve Champagne or Champagne cocktails. However, the flute helps to preserve the fizz

(2) Highball/Collins glass
Tall tumblers used to serve long, ice-filled drinks with soda or fruit juice. The Collins is slightly larger than the highball

(3) Cocktail/Martini glass
This is the classic symbol of cocktail culture. Elegant, cool and sophisticated, the conical bowl on a tall stem is traditionally used for Martinis

(3)

(1)

(5)

(4) Tumbler/rocks glass
Short, sturdy glasses used for serving drinks over ice, or 'on the rocks'

(5) Shot glass
Very small glass used for consuming (or measuring) shots of spirit

(6) Wine glasses
Various sizes are useful for wine and different types of cocktails. Long stems help to keep warm hands away from your chilled drink

Techniques

Crushing ice

Many cocktails use crushed ice or "ice snow" as an ingredient. You must crush ice before using it in a blender

(1) Place a tea towel on a counter and partly cover it with ice cubes. Fold the cloth over the cubes

(2) Using a hammer, hit the ice firmly to crush it

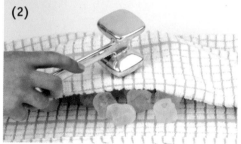

(3) Spoon the ice pieces into your glasses or mixing jug. Large pieces can be stored in bags in the freezer, but the fine "ice snow" must be used immediately

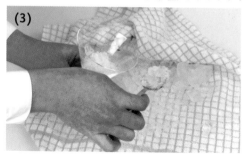

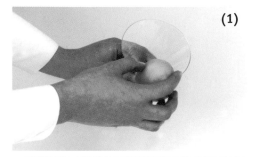

(1)

Frosted glasses

Many types of cocktails are enhanced by being served in a glass with a frosted rim. Salt or sugar are typically used, but you could create your own

(1) Holding the glass upside-down, rub the rim with the cut surface of lemon, orange or other suitable fruit

(2)

(2) Dip the rim in a shallow layer of the sugar or salt. Make sure the rim is well coated

(3) Leave the glass upright until the rim is dry. Chill in the refrigerator if necessary

(3)

Essentials and Tips

Flavorings
Essential cocktail flavorings include hot pepper sauce, Worcestershire sauce and Angostura bitters

Garnishes
Colorful and tasty garnishes can really make a difference to a cocktail. They should be fresh and of good quality. Cherries, lemons, limes and pineapples are common for sweet drinks; drier tastes may be finished with olives, celery or onions

Glasses
Make sure glasses are washed, dried and very clean. Never serve a cocktail in a warm glass — chill it in the refrigerator if necessary

Ice
Do not be afraid to use lots of ice. It keeps the drink cooler for a lot longer

Measures

An extra-large measure of alcohol does not improve a cocktail. Keep to the amounts shown in the recipes for reasons of class and authenticity. If you need more alcohol, mix up another cocktail!

Mixers

Always use the best mixers that you can afford. For juices, fresh is definitely best and make sure creams are not past their best. Some essential mixers include: cranberry, lemon, orange, lime, tomato and pineapple juices, cola and tonic water

Sweeteners

Fine sugar mixes into drinks well or even better make, or buy, some sugar syrup

Twist or slice?

A twist is a small strip of lemon or lime peel. Squeezing the twist over the drink will release the oils from the peel. Do not make slices too thick or thin

Contents

Applesinthe

Glass: Highball

Ingredients:
1.5 measure absinthe
Half a teaspoon of sugar syrup
One teaspoon of passion fruit syrup
1 measure fresh lemon juice
0.5 measure apple schnapps
2 measures fresh apple juice
Dash of orange bitters

Method:
Shake ingredients and strain over crushed ice into a highball

Garnish:
With slices or wedges of apple

B-52

Glass: Tumbler

Ingredients:
0.5 measure chocolate liqueur
0.5 measure Irish cream
0.5 measure cognac-based orange liqueur

Method:
Shake the ingredients together and pour over ice into a tumbler glass

Between the Sheets

Glass: Cocktail

Ingredients:
1 measure brandy
1 measure orange liqueur
1 measure white rum
0.5 measure fresh lemon juice

Method:
Shake ingredients with ice and strain into a chilled cocktail glass

Garnish:
With a long lemon zest twist

Black Russian*

Glass: Tumbler

Ingredients:
2 measures vodka
1 measure chocolate liqueur

Method:
Pour the ingredients over ice into a tumbler glass

Garnish:
With cherries

You can turn the Black Russian into a Long Black Russian by changing the glass to a highball and topping the drink with cola

Black Velvet

Glass: Wine

Ingredients:
Champagne
Irish stout

Method:
Half fill a wine glass with the Irish stout
and top up with Champagne

Blood & Sand

Glass: Cocktail

Ingredients:
1.25 measure Scotch whisky
1 measure cherry liqueur
1 measure sweet vermouth
1 measure fresh orange juice

Method:
Shake ingredients with ice and strain into
a chilled cocktail glass

Garnish:
With an orange slice

Bloody Mary

Glass: Highball

Ingredients:
2 measure vodka
6 fl oz tomato juice
Freshly squeezed juice of a lemon
Pinch of salt and pepper
One to three dashes of hot pepper sauce
Half a teaspoon of horseradish
Four to six dashes of Worcestershire sauce
Pinch of celery salt

Method:
Shake all the ingredients together with a scoop of ice

Garnish:
Serve in a highball glass garnished with a lemon slice and a stick of celery

Blue Hawaiian

Glass: Wine

Ingredients:
2 measures white rum
1 measure blue curaçao
3.5 fl oz pineapple juice
2 measures cream of coconut
Crushed ice

Method:
Add ingredients to a blender and mix for
20-30 seconds, pour into a wine glass

Garnish:
With a pineapple wedge and a cocktail
umbrella

Bucks Fizz*

Glass: Flute

Ingredients:
1.5-3.5 fl oz freshly-squeezed orange juice
Champagne

Method:
Pour the orange juice into a flute and top with chilled dry Champagne

Also known as the Mimosa

Caipirinha

Glass: Tumbler

Ingredients:
2 measures cachaca
One lime
Two brown sugar cubes

Method:
Cut the lime into eights and place into a tumbler glass with the sugar cubes and swirl together. Fill the glass with crushed ice and top with cachaca and stir

Garnish:
With a wedge of lime

Champagne Cocktail*

Glass: Flute

Ingredients:
1 measure brandy
One white sugar cube
Angostura bitters
Champagne

Method:
Cover the sugar cube in Angostura bitters and place into a flute. Add the brandy and top with Champagne

This Cocktail is also known as the Classic Champagne Cocktail and sometimes the Business Brace

Cosmopolitan

Glass: Cocktail

Ingredients:
2 measures lemon vodka
1 measure orange liqueur
Dash of cranberry juice
Squeeze of fresh lime

Method:
Shake and strain into a chilled
cocktail glass

Garnish:
With flamed lime zest

Daiquiri (original)

Glass: Highball

Ingredients:
2 measures golden rum
0.5 measure fresh lime juice
0.5 measure sugar syrup

Method:
Shake with ice and strain into a
highball glass over fresh ice

Garnish:
With a twisted slice of lime or serve in a
sugar frosted glass

Egg Nog

Glass: Tumbler

Ingredients:
1 measure brandy
1 measure dark rum
One egg white
One teaspoon of sugar
Milk
Nutmeg

Method:
Shake all ingredients (except milk) with ice. Strain into a tumbler glass. Top up with milk

Garnish:
With a sprinkle of nutmeg

Fuzzy Navel

Glass: Tumbler

Ingredients:
2 measures peach schnapps
Orange juice

Method:
Pour the peach schnapps over ice. Top up with orange juice

Garnish:
With an orange slice

Gimlet

Glass: Cocktail

Ingredients:
2 measures gin
1 measure lime cordial
One lime wedge

Method:
Pour gin and lime cordial into a shaker with ice, squeeze in the lime juice and add the wedge. Shake and strain into a cocktail glass

Garnish:
With a slice of lime and a cherry or served in a frosted cocktail glass

Grasshopper

Glass: Cocktail

Ingredients:
1 measure white creme de cacao
1 measure green creme de menthe
1 measure fresh cream

Method:
Shake ingredients vigorously and strain
into a cocktail glass

Garnish:
With cherries and a sprig of mint

Harvey Wallbanger

Glass: Highball

Ingredients:
1 measure vodka
0.5 measure galliano
Fresh orange juice

Method:
Into a highball filled with ice, pour the vodka and orange juice. Then float the galliano on the top

Garnish:
With an orange slice

Hawaiian

Glass: Cocktail

Ingredients:
2 measures gin
0.5 measure triple sec
0.5 measure pineapple juice

Method:
Shake all the ingredients together with some crushed ice. Strain and pour

Garnish:
With cherries and an orange slice

Income Tax

Glass: Tumbler

Ingredients:
2 measures of gin
0.5 measure of dry vermouth
1 measure of orange juice
Two or three dashes of bitters

Method:
Shake all the ingredients with the crushed ice. Strain and pour over fresh ice

Garnish:
With a slice of orange

Jamaican Slammer

Glass: Shot

Ingredients:
0.5 measure golden rum
0.5 measure triple sec
0.5 measure dark rum
Five drops of lime juice

Method: Pour the dark rum into the shot glass. Next float the triple sec and then add the lime juice before floating the golden rum on top

John Collins

Glass: Highball

Ingredients:
2 measures whisky
1 measure lemon juice
Dash of sugar syrup
Soda water

Method:
Shake the whisky, lemon juice and sugar syrup along with crushed ice. Strain and pour over more ice. Top up with soda water and stir gently

Garnish:
With orange and lemon segments and a cherry

Kir Royale

Glass: Flute

Ingredients:
0.5 measure creme de cassis
Champagne

Method:
Pour the cassis into a flute and top with chilled Champagne

Long Island Iced Tea

Glass: Highball

Ingredients:
0.5 measure vodka
0.5 measure gin
0.5 measure white rum
0.5 measure tequila
0.5 measure triple sec
1 measure fresh lemon juice
Dash of sugar syrup
Cola

Method:
Build ingredients over ice into a highball glass, top with cola

Garnish:
With a slice of lime

Mai Tai

Glass: Highball

Ingredients:
2 measures rum
0.5 measure orange curaçao
0.5 measure apricot brandy
0.5 measure fresh lime juice
0.5 measure pineapple juice
Dash of Angostura bitters
Two dashes of orgeat syrup

Method:
Shake all ingredients with ice and strain
into an ice-filled highball glass

Garnish:
With a twist of orange

Manhattan

Glass: Cocktail

Ingredients:
2 measures whisky
1 measure sweet vermouth
Dash of Angostura bitters
A cherry to garnish

Method:
Stir together with ice, strain into a cocktail glass

Garnish:
With a cherry

Margarita

Glass: Cocktail

Ingredients:
1 measure gold tequila
1 measure triple sec
1 measure fresh lime juice

Method:
Frost the rim of the glass with salt.
Shake all the ingredients with cracked ice.
Strain and pour into the salt frosted glass

Martini (dry)

Glass: Cocktail

Ingredients:
2 measures gin
0.5 measure dry vermouth
Green olives or lemon zest

Method:
Pre-chill your glass, fill the mixing jug with ice, add the pre-chilled ingredients in the required ratios. Stir quickly and smoothly for approximately ten seconds and then pour into the chilled glass

Garnish:
Serve with olives or a strip of lemon zest

Metropolitan

Glass: Cocktail

Ingredients:
2 measures brandy
1 measure sweet vermouth
A dash of Angostura bitters

Method:
Coat the glass with the angostura bitters.
Shake the brandy and vermouth with
cracked ice. Strain and pour into a chilled
cocktail glass

Garnish:
With a cherry

Mojito

Glass: Highball

Ingredients:
2 measures light rum
Four white cane sugar cubes
(or dash of sugar syrup)
Seven or eight fresh mint leaves
A sliced and diced lime
Soda water

Method:
Muddle the mint, sugar and lime in a
highball, then fill the glass with crushed
ice, pour the rum, top up with soda
and stir

Garnish:
With a sprig of mint and twist of lime

Moscow Mule

Glass: Highball

Ingredients:
2 measures vodka
1 measure fresh lime
Ginger beer

Method:
Build ingredients over ice into a highball glass

Garnish:
With a wedge of lime

Nelson's Blood

Glass: Flute

Ingredients:
1 measure ruby port
Champagne

Method:
Pour ingredients into a champagne flute

October Revolution

Glass: Highball

Ingredients:
2 measures vodka
2 measures coffee liqueur
2 measures creme de cacao
2 measures double cream

Method:
Shake ingredients with ice, strain into a
highball glass containing ice

Garnish:
Serve with a straw

Pina Colada

Glass: Highball

Ingredients:
2 measures golden rum
1 measure cream
1 measure coconut milk
2 measures pineapple juice

Method:
Shake ingredients with ice and strain over ice into a highball glass

Garnish:
With a pineapple wedge and a cocktail umbrella

Pink Gin

Glass: Tumbler

Ingredients:
2 measures gin
Dash of Angostura bitters

Method:
Pour ingredients over ice into a tumbler
glass and stir to chill

Garnish:
Squeeze in oils from a lemon zest and use
a slice of lemon as garnish

Pink Lady*

Glass: Cocktail

Ingredients:
1 measure gin
1 measure orange liqueur
1 measure fresh lemon juice
Dash of egg white (optional)
Dash of grenadine

Method:
Shake ingredients with ice and strain into
a chilled cocktail glass

*To change into a White Lady take out the
dash of grenadine*

Red, White & Blue

Glass: Shot

Ingredients:
0.5 measure grenadine
0.5 measure peach schnapps
0.5 measure blue curaçao

Method:
Pour the grenadine. Next float the peach schnapps, then the blue curaçao

This cocktail works better if you chill the ingredients beforehand

Rob Roy

Glass: Cocktail

Ingredients:
1.5 measure Scotch whisky
1 measure sweet vermouth
A dash of Angostura bitters

Method:
Add ingredients to an ice-filled mixing glass and stir until chilled. Strain into a cocktail glass

Garnish:
Garnish with lemon zest and a cherry

Make a Dry Rob Roy by replacing the sweet vermouth with a dry vermouth and make a perfect Rob Roy by using half sweet and half dry vermouths

Rusty Nail

Glass: Tumbler

Ingredients:
1 measure whisky
1 measure drambuie

Method:
Pour ingredients over ice into a tumbler glass

Garnish:
With a slice of orange

Sea Breeze

Glass: Highball

Ingredients:
2 measures vodka
5 fl oz cranberry juice
2 measures grapefruit juice

Method:
Build over ice into a highball glass

Garnish:
With a lime slice

Sex on the Beach

Glass: Highball

Ingredients:
1 measure vodka
1 measure peach schnapps
7 fl oz fresh cranberry juice
3.5 fl oz orange juice

Method:
Shake ingredients with ice and strain into
a highball filled with fresh ice

Garnish:
With orange or lime slices

Singapore Sling

Glass: Tumbler

Ingredients:
2 measures gin
1 measure cherry brandy
1 tsp sugar syrup
0.5 measure fresh lime juice
Soda water

Method:
Shake ingredients with ice and pour into a tumbler glass filled with ice. Top with soda water

Garnish:
With a slice of lime

Thin Blue Line

Glass: Shot

Ingredients:
0.5 measure of triple sec
0.5 measure of vodka
Four or five drops of blue curaçao

Method:
Pour the triple sec and float the vodka carefully over the top of it. Then, with a straw or dropper, add the curaçao drops

This cocktail works better if you chill the ingredients beforehand

Tokyo Silver Fizz

Glass: Highball

Ingredients:
1 measure vodka
1 measure melon liqueur
0.5 measure lemon juice
Dash of egg white
Soda water

Method:
Shake ingredients (except soda) and strain over fresh ice into a highball. Top with soda water

Garnish:
Top with a lemon slice

Vodkatini

Glass: Cocktail

Ingredients:
2 measures vodka
A dash of dry vermouth

Method:
Stir the vermouth and vodka with ice in a pre-chilled mixing glass. Stir until chilled and strain into a chilled cocktail glass

Garnish:
With a pitted olive or lemon zest

Whisky Sour

Glass: Tumbler

Ingredients:
2 measures of whisky
1 measure of lemon juice
1 measure of sugar syrup

Method:
Mix the ingredients in a tumbler glass over ice

Garnish:
With a twist of lemon

White Russian

Glass: Tumbler

Ingredients:
2 measures vodka
1 measure chocolate liqueur
1 measure single cream

Method:
Pour vodka and the chocolate liqueur into a tumbler glass filled with ice. Layer the cream on top

Garnish:
With a stemmed cherry

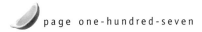

Xantippe

Glass: Cocktail

Ingredients:
2 measures vodka
1 measure yellow chartreuse
1 measure cherry brandy

Method:
Stir the ingredients vigorously with ice.
Strain into a chilled cocktail glass

Yellow Ribbon

Glass: Tumbler

Ingredients:
2 measures mandarin vodka
1 measure lemon juice
0.5 measure frangelico
0.5 measure sugar syrup

Method:
Shake and strain into a tumbler glass

Garnish:
With a lemon wedge

Zombie

Glass: Highball

Ingredients:
1 measure lemon juice
2 teaspoons of grenadine
2 dashes of Angostura bitters
1 measure spiced rum
7 fl oz orange juice
1 measure apricot brandy
3.5 fl oz guava/mango/other exotic juices
1 measure light rum
0.5 measure "float" of dark rum

Method:
In a highball glass pour the ingredients
in order as above

Garnish:
With lemon and lime slices

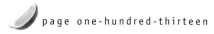

Non-alcoholic cocktails

Non-alcoholic cocktails allow drivers, teetotalers and children to join in with the fun spirit of a cocktail without the obvious side effects that the alcoholic versions have

Often vibrantly fruity and refreshing, and with equally exotic mixes of ingredients, you'll hardly notice the difference as you sample the delights of a Brown Horny Toad, a Honeymoon or maybe a Starburst. These cocktails can be enjoyed any time of day, in any situation.

Brown Horny Toad

Glass: Highball

2 measures pineapple juice
2 measures orange juice
1 measure lemon juice
One teaspoon grenadine
One teaspoon sugar syrup
Pinch of ground cinnamon
Pinch of ground cloves

Method:
Shake ingredients with ice and strain over
fresh ice into a highball

Garnish:
With an orange and lemon slice

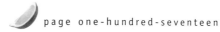

Caribbean Cocktail

Glass: Tumbler

Ingredients:
Fresh mango (peeled)
A banana
Juice of an orange
A dash of fresh lime juice

Method:
Blend the mango and banana with the
juices and a few ice cubes until smooth.
Strain over fresh ice into a tumbler

Garnish:
With slices of banana and a
cocktail umbrella

Honeymoon

Glass: Cocktail

Ingredients:
1 measure clear honey
0.5 measure fresh lime juice
1 measure orange juice
1 measure apple juice

Method:
Shake ingredients with crushed ice and strain into a cocktail glass

Garnish:
With a cherry

San Francisco

Glass: Wine

Ingredients:
1 measure fresh orange juice
1 measure fresh lemon juice
1 measure fresh pineapple juice
1 measure fresh grapefruit juice
0.5 measure grenadine
A dash of egg white
Soda water

Method:
Shake ingredients (apart from soda)
with ice and strain over fresh ice into a
wine glass and top up with soda water

Garnish:
With lemon, lime and orange slices

Starburst

Glass: Highball

Ingredients:
1 banana
1 kiwi
10 fresh strawberries
5 fl oz apple juice
Crushed ice

Method:
Slice fruit and place into a blender
with apple juice. After blending pour into
a highball

Garnish:
With strawberries

Glossary

All of the ingredients needed to make the cocktails in this book are listed

Absinthe
Infamous, very powerful spirit. Said to have hallucinogenic properties

Angostura bitters
Bitter flavoring derived from tree bark

Apple juice

Apple schnapps

Apricot brandy

Banana

Blackcurrant vodka
Vodka with a twist of blackcurrant

Blue curaçao
Blue colored liqueur flavored with orange peel

Brandy

Cachaca
White Brazilian rum made from sugar cane

Celery

Celery salt

Champagne

Cherries

Cherry brandy

Chocolate dust
Powdered chocolate for garnishing

Coconut cream	Gin
Coffee liqueur	Ginger beer
Cognac-based orange liqueur	Golden rum
Cola	Grapefruit juice
Cranberry juice	Green olives
Cream *Single and double*	Grenadine *Syrup derived from pomegranates*
Cream of coconut	Ground cinnamon
Creme de cacao *Brandy-based cream liqueur with cacao*	Ground cloves
Creme de cassis *Brandy-based cream liqueur with blackcurrants*	Guava juice
	Horseradish
Creme de menthe *Brandy-based cream liqueur with mint*	Hot pepper sauce
	Ice
Dark rum	Irish stout
Drambuie *Whisky flavored with honey and herbs*	Kiwi
	Lemon juice
Eggs	Lemons
Frangelico *Hazelnut liqueur*	Lemon vodka *Vodka with a twist of lemon*
	Light rum
	Lime juice

Limes

Mandarin vodka
Vodka with a twist of orange

Mango

Mango juice

Maraschino cherries

Melon liqueur

Milk

Mint leaves

Nutmeg

Orange bitters

Orange curaçao
Orange colored liqueur flavored with orange peel

Orange juice

Orange liqueur

Oranges

Passion syrup

Peach schnapps

Pepper

Pineapple

Pineapple juice

Ruby Port

Rum-based coffee liqueur

Salt

Soda water

Spiced rum

Sugar cubes
Brown and white

Sugar syrup

Tequila

Tomato juice

Triple sec
Sweet, white colored curaçao

Vermouth dry

Vermouth sweet

Vodka

Whisky
Irish, Scotch and Rye

Worcestershire sauce

Yellow chartreuse
Liqueur flavored with orange and myrtle